WN

Brook Street

Black Diamond Street

Station Road

CHESTER

Hoole Way

Brook Street

Francis Street

Crewe Street

Egerton Street

City Road

Milton Street

Leadworks Lane

St Oswald's Way

on Terrace

Canal Side

Canal Side

BOUGHTON SHOT TOWER

Phillip Street

Faulkner Street

HOOLE PARK

Crawford's Walk

Hoole Park

Westminster Road

Lightfoot Street

Hoole Lane

Hoole Lane

Spital Walk

The Bars

Boughton

BOUGHTON

EASTGATE BRIDGE

Vicar's Lane

Grosvenor Park Road

Grosvenor Park

River Dee

the Groves

Victoria Crescent

Queen's Drive

Elizabeth Crescent

QUEEN'S PARK

Edinburgh Way

St George's Crescent

Queen's Park Road

Bottoms Lane

Meadows Lane

D0542678

Key

Train station

Bus station

School

Church

Information

children's HISTORY of
CHESTER

Written by
Tony Pickford

Waltons

HOMETOWN WORLD

How well do you know your town?

Have you ever wondered what it would have been like to go to Chester's amphitheatre in Roman times? Or how and why the Rows were built? This book will uncover the important and exciting things that happened in your town.

Want to hear the other good bits? You will love this book! Some rather brainy folk have worked on it to make sure it's fun and informative. So what are you waiting for? Peel back the pages and be amazed at the story behind your very own town.

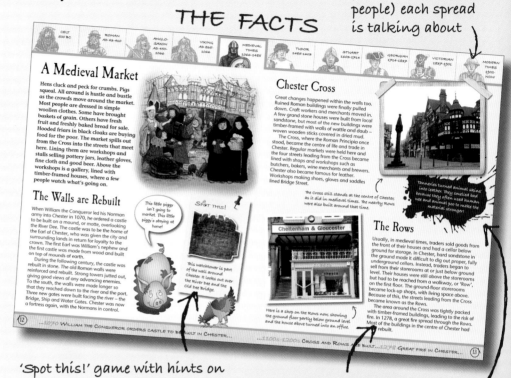

Timeline shows which period (dates and people) each spread is talking about

'Spot this!' game with hints on something to find in your town

Clear informative text

Hometown facts to amaze you!

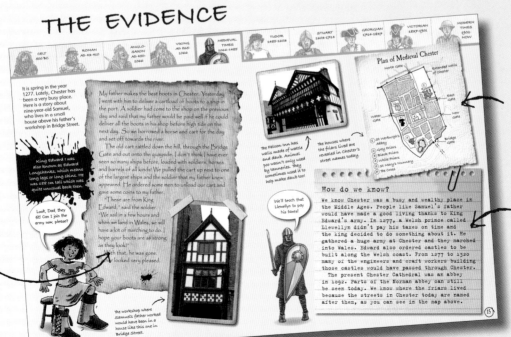

Go back in time to read what it was like for children growing up in Chester

Intriguing maps and photos

Each period in the book ends with a summary explaining how we know about the past

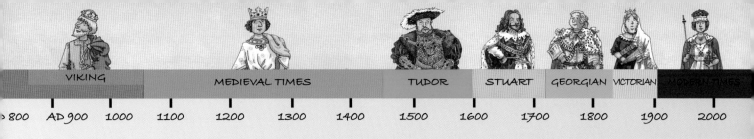

Contents

CELT
500 BC

ROMAN
AD 43-410

ANGLO-
SAXON
AD 450-
1066

VIKING
AD 865-
1066

MEDIEV
TIME.
1066
1485

A Roman Fortress

Darkness is falling and the wind is blowing in from the sea. A line of eighty soldiers marches into the fortress. Their round helmets and curved shields gleam in the light of flaming torches high on the walls. Red cloaks are wrapped tightly around their shoulders to protect them from the winter chill. It has been a long march today, from the copper mines in the hills to the south, which they have been protecting from thieves. For some of the soldiers, this foreign land is very different from their warm and sunny homeland. For others, this place is now their home.

The Romans Arrive!

The Roman army came to Britain in AD 43. They gradually moved north and took over the lands of Celtic tribes, sometimes peacefully through displays of their strength, and sometimes after fierce battles.

The Romans arrived in Chester around AD 48. They found a flat-topped hill overlooking a bend in the River Dee as it neared the sea. They called this place Deva. It was an ideal site for a fortress with good views across the river valley. It would be a base for further victories, easily supplied by sea, and home for a Legion of around 5,000 men.

At first a small timber fort was built, but by the year AD 88, when the Twentieth Legion moved in, it was being replaced by a much larger, grander fortress with walls and buildings made of local sandstone.

This painting from the Grosvenor Museum shows us what Roman Chester might have looked like.

Four Walls and a Fortress

Like other fortresses across the Roman Empire, Deva was laid out in the shape of a playing card. Surrounded by stone walls nearly 7 metres high, it had gates in each of its four sides and at the centre, where roads met, stood a headquarters building or Principia – where a special flag called the Standard of the Legion was stored. Most of the other buildings in the fortress were barracks for the soldiers, though there was a large house, called a Praetorium, for the commander of the Legion, a hospital, a bathhouse and shrines to Roman gods.

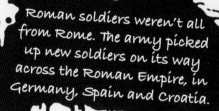

Roman soldiers weren't all from Rome. The army picked up new soldiers on its way across the Roman Empire, in Germany, Spain and Croatia.

I'm 100 per cent Roman and I've got the nose to prove it!

This roof tile is from the Roman army barracks in Deva.

At Chester's Roman Gardens, you can see what a real Roman hypocaust looked like.

SPOT THIS!

The Roman Gardens in Chester can be found between Pepper Street and the Groves. Look out for this once fiery furnace!

Central Heating

Deva must have seemed a cold place to the well-travelled soldiers. Several buildings in the fortress had an early kind of central heating. The Principia, for example, had hollow walls and a raised floor supported by stone columns. In the corner of the building was a furnace, in which a fire was lit. Holes or vents in the walls led to chimneys, which carried heat from the fire under the floors and throughout the rest of the building. This type of heating was called a hypocaust.

Heating would have been especially welcome in the bathhouse, where soldiers went to relax and chat, as well as get themselves clean. The bathhouse would have had a hypocaust.

The Amphitheatre

Where is everyone? Soldiers tramp along the walls on guard duty, but the streets, shops and workshops are strangely quiet. Cheering and clapping suddenly echoes from the amphitheatre. Inside its 12 metre high walls, thousands of people are crammed into seats overlooking a circular arena. A few latecomers stop at the stalls around the entrance to buy snacks. It seems like the whole of Deva is here. The crowd is watching as men on horseback hunt wild beasts. Bears growl and wild boars grunt and squeal. Later, beasts will be let loose on traitors to Rome!

Release the lions!

A Stone Stadium

The amphitheatre in Deva began as a simple wooden building. It was soon rebuilt in stone to seat up to 8,000 people. As well as a place where soldiers could practise their marching and combat skills, it was the scene of hunts and fights between animals such as bears and dogs.

An amphitheatre was the centre of life in any Roman town. For a fortress like Deva, it was a strong symbol of Roman culture and power. There were battles between gladiators and public executions of criminals and traitors.

In the middle of the second century, the Twentieth Legion was sent north from Deva to help build Hadrian's Wall and the amphitheatre was no longer used. The fortress must have been very quiet at this time, with just a few soldiers left behind to guard it and organise the sending of supplies north by sea.

The Roman amphitheatre in Deva could seat 8,000 people!

Show Time

When the Twentieth Legion returned, however, the amphitheatre was improved. The arena was lowered and the seating was put on top of steep banks to give better views for spectators. A large stone with an iron ring was placed in the centre of the arena for tying up the animal or human victims of hunts and executions. The amphitheatre held lots of different shows, ceremonies and sights – a cross between a modern theatre, sports stadium and circus!

Whoever made this helmet must have got carried away with the eyeholes!

SPOT THIS!

This tombstone was found in the north wall in Chester and shows a Sarmatian cavalryman. You can see it at Grosvenor Museum.

Sarmatians came from eastern Europe and were beaten by the Romans. Sarmatian horsemen carried special flags which made a hissing noise in the wind!

This coin dates from around AD 341 to 346, the time of Emperor Constantius. Experts think it could be forged, or fake.

This was found in the amphitheatre. It is a carved piece of animal bone and was part of a Roman sword handle.

A Trading Town

By the year AD 150, a town had grown outside the walls of the fortress. Local people settled here to trade. Later, after AD 212, when the law was changed to let soldiers get married, soldiers' families moved in. An inn or 'mansio', with rooms for travellers to stay, stood to the south on the road leading down to the river. Secure warehouses were built here to store goods, like wine and olive oil, being taken in and out of the port.

There were houses and shops selling food, wine and pottery in the area of what is now Foregate Street. Workshops produced ironwork, bricks, tiles and jewellery. There was a bathhouse, like the one inside the fortress. Across the river, there was a shrine to the goddess Minerva and a busy yard where boats and ships were built. By AD 230 the streets of Deva would have been lined with stone and brick buildings with roofs made of red clay tiles.

CELT
500 BC

ROMAN
AD 43-410

ANGLO-
SAXON
AD 450-
1066

VIKING
AD 865-
1066

MEDIEV
TIMES
1066-
1485

Antilianus is 10 years old. He has lived in the town outside the fortress walls all his life. His mother married a soldier and Antilianus wants to join the Legion himself when he grows up. Here is an imaginary story from Antilianus.

Today my friend Seutonius and I saw a sight that made us laugh! We were playing dice in the street near the tilemaker's workshop. Suddenly we heard shouting coming from the workshop and the sound of running feet. We turned to see what was going on and saw a small, brown, scruffy dog dash out of the door and away down the street.

A moment later, the tilemaker appeared at his door, shouting and cursing at the dog. He seemed so cross, we didn't dare ask what was wrong! We guessed that the dog must have done some damage, so we picked up our dice and sneaked round the back of the workshop to take a look. We peered over the wall into the tilemaker's yard where he puts out his clay roof tiles to dry in the sun.

There were rows of tiles laid out and the ones nearest the workshop, which were obviously still quite wet, had the dog's footprints all over them. It looked like the dog had been dancing on them! Perhaps he had been chasing something. Seutonius and I looked at each other and got the giggles! Just then, the tilemaker appeared again, so we ran away.

If you throw another double six, I'll throw you to the lions!

These dice made of animal bone are in the Grosvenor Museum.

TUDOR
1485-1603

STUART
1603-1714

GEORGIAN
1714-1837

VICTORIAN
1837-1901

MODERN
TIMES
1902-NOW

It wasn't me, Mr Angry
Roman Tilemaker, sir!

One of the most interesting
objects in the Education
Room of the Grosvenor
Museum is a piece of a
Roman roof tile with the
imprint of a dog's paw!

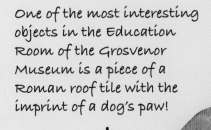

The Romans used
clay to make things
like jugs and pots,
as well as roof tiles.

How do we know?

The Newstead Gallery at the Grosvenor Museum
in Chester is full of objects from Roman times
including jewellery and pottery. The Roman
collection also has some tiny locks and keys,
like ones we might use today on a suitcase.
You can even see a set of dice like the ones
Antilianus might have played with.

The amphitheatre in Chester also tells us a
lot about life in Roman times. It lay buried
for centuries until it was rediscovered in
1929: a house that had been built on the site
of the amphitheatre was having some building
work done, when the discovery was made.
Archaeologists dug down into the remains
and found some of the everyday objects left
behind by the crowds at the amphitheatre.

Outside the fortress walls in Roman
times was a cemetery for both soldiers and
citizens. Roman tombstones gave information
about the person who was buried, often in the
form of carvings. Many are displayed in the
Grosvenor Museum, along with lots of other
Roman artefacts.

CELT 500 BC	ROMAN AD 43-410	ANGLO-SAXON AD 450-1066	VIKING AD 865-1066	MEDIEV TIMES 1066 1485

Invaders in Longships

It is early morning on a frosty winter's day and mist is rising from the river. The strong walls of Chester's fortress still stand, but have been patched up with stones and banks of earth. Inside the walls, some buildings have crumbled and others have been roughly repaired. Behind their defences, soldiers huddle together against the cold. They are wearing coarse woollen clothes with cloaks and furs to keep them warm. As they guard the walls, mighty Viking longships move along the misty river towards the shore.

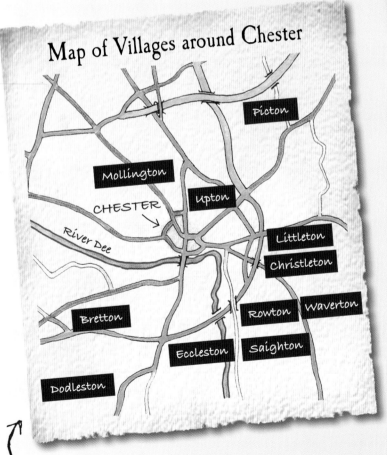

Map of Villages around Chester

Picton

Mollington

CHESTER

Upton

River Dee

Littleton

Christleton

Bretton

Rowton   Waverton

Eccleston   Saighton

Dodleston

This map shows villages around Chester whose names end in 'ton'. These could have been Saxon villages.

After the Romans

In the 4th century, invaders were threatening the Roman Empire. Some time after the year AD 380, the Roman Legion left Chester for good, probably to help defend the Empire's borders in eastern Europe. The people left behind would have been used to the Roman lifestyle, so this must have been a terrible blow.

Life in Chester centred on the town outside the walls. Trade carried on from the port, but in the 5th and 6th centuries, the population fell. At this time, settlers from northern Europe called Saxons moved into the area and built many nearby villages. The names of these places tell us that the Saxons were Christians – Christleton means village of the Christians. West Cheshire has lots of places ending in 'ton' – the Saxon word for a village.

A Saxon Kingdom

By the year AD 689, Chester was part of the Saxon kingdom of Mercia. King Ethelred founded the church of St John the Baptist close to the site of the Roman amphitheatre. Saxon Chester was mainly made up of timber buildings with thatched roofs. The fortress was left to decay and both the commander's house and the bathhouse collapsed around this time.

Vikings, Keep Out!

In the late 9th century, Chester must have been a strange place – a derelict fortress with a thriving town outside. In AD 893, another army of invaders and settlers arrived and stayed for a while in the deserted fortress. These were Vikings from Scandinavia, who had taken over much of northern and eastern England, an area known as the Danelaw. Chester was one of very few places left in northern England still held by the Saxons and they fought hard to keep the Vikings out.

Viking helmets didn't have horns as many people used to think. Horns would have been dangerous, risking injury to men fighting on the same side.

This stained-glass window in a Gloucestershire church shows Ethelfleda, the queen of Mercia.

Queen Ethelfleda

Only one whole Saxon kingdom stayed strong against the Viking threat – Wessex, in the south west of England, led by its king, Alfred the Great. Ethelfleda, Alfred's daughter, became queen of Mercia. She decided to set up some strong, defended settlements, called burhs, to keep the Vikings out. Chester was one of those burhs.

Ethelfleda died in AD 918, after founding the church of St Peter, which still stands at the Cross. Behind the strong defences, Chester became a successful town, which minted its own coins. What the Vikings had failed to do by force soon began to happen in other ways, however. Because of trade with Viking places, such as Dublin, many Viking families settled near the port.

SPOT THIS!

St Peter's was built on the site of the old Roman Praetorium, where the commander lived. It's made from red sandstone. Do you know where it is?

CELT
500 BC

ROMAN
AD 43-410

ANGLO-
SAXON
AD 450-
1066

VIKING
AD 865-
1066

MEDIEVAL
TIMES
1066-14

A Medieval Market

Hens cluck and peck for crumbs. Pigs squeal. All around is hustle and bustle as the crowds move around the market. Most people are dressed in simple woollen clothes. Some have brought baskets of grain. Others have fresh fruit and freshly baked bread for sale. Hooded friars in black cloaks are buying food for the poor. The market spills out from the Cross into the streets that meet here. Lining them are workshops and stalls selling pottery jars, leather gloves, fine cloth and good beer. Above the workshops is a gallery, lined with timber-framed houses, where a few people watch what's going on.

The Walls are Rebuilt

When William the Conqueror led his Norman army into Chester in 1070, he ordered a castle to be built on a mound, or motte, overlooking the River Dee. The castle was to be the home of the Earl of Chester, who was given the city and surrounding lands in return for loyalty to the crown. The first Earl was William's nephew and the first castle was made from wood and built on top of mounds of earth.

During the following century, the castle was rebuilt in stone. The old Roman walls were reinforced and rebuilt. Strong towers jutted out, giving good views of any advancing enemies. To the south, the walls were made longer so that they reached down to the river and the port. Three new gates were built facing the river – the Bridge, Ship and Water Gates. Chester was now a fortress again, with the Normans in control.

This little piggy isn't going to market. This little piggy's staying at home!

SPOT THIS!

This watchtower is part of the wall around Chester. It looks out over the River Dee and the Old Dee Bridge.

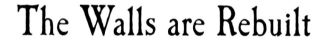

Chester Cross

Great changes happened within the walls too. Ruined Roman buildings were finally pulled down. Craft workers and merchants moved in. A few grand stone houses were built from local sandstone, but most of the new buildings were timber-framed with walls of wattle and daub – woven wooden sticks covered in dried mud.

The Cross, where the Roman Principia once stood, became the centre of life and trade in Chester. Regular markets were held here and the four streets leading from the Cross became lined with shops and workshops such as butchers, bakers, wine merchants and brewers. Chester also became famous for leather. Workshops making shoes, gloves and saddles lined Bridge Street.

The Cross still stands at the centre of Chester, as it did in medieval times. The nearby Rows were also built around that time.

Tanneries turned animal skins into leather. They smelled bad because they often used human wee and animal poo to make the material stronger!

Here is a shop on the Rows now, showing the ground floor partly below ground level and the house above turned into an office.

The Rows

Usually, in medieval times, traders sold goods from the front of their houses and had a cellar below ground for storage. In Chester, hard sandstone in the ground made it difficult to dig out proper, fully underground cellars. Instead, traders began to sell from their storerooms at or just below ground level. Their houses were still above the storerooms but had to be reached from a walkway, or 'Row', on the first floor. The ground-floor storerooms became lock-up shops, with living space above. Because of this, the streets leading from the Cross became known as the Rows.

The area around the Cross was tightly packed with timber-framed buildings, leading to the risk of fire. In 1278, a great fire spread through the Rows. Most of the buildings in the centre of Chester had to be rebuilt.

It is spring in the year 1277. Lately, Chester has been a very busy place. Here is a story about nine-year-old Samuel, who lives in a small house above his father's workshop in Bridge Street.

King Edward I was also known as Edward Longshanks, which means long legs or long shins. He was 188 cm tall which was quite unusual back then.

Look, Dad, they fit! Can I join the army now, please?

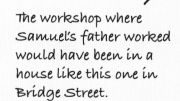

My father makes the best boots in Chester. Yesterday I went with him to deliver a cartload of boots to a ship in the port. A soldier had come to the shop on the previous day and said that my father would be paid well if he could deliver all the boots in his shop before high tide on the next day. So we borrowed a horse and cart for the day and set off towards the river.

The old cart rattled down the hill, through the Bridge Gate and out onto the quayside. I don't think I have ever seen so many ships before, loaded with soldiers, horses and barrels of all kinds! We pulled the cart up next to one of the largest ships and the soldier that my father knew appeared. He ordered some men to unload our cart and gave some coins to my father.

"These are from King Edward," said the soldier. "We sail in a few hours and when we land in Wales, we will have a lot of marching to do. I hope your boots are as strong as they look!"

With that, he was gone. Father looked very pleased.

The workshop where Samuel's father worked would have been in a house like this one in Bridge Street.

TUDOR
1485-1603

STUART
1603-1714

GEORGIAN
1714-1837

VICTORIAN
1837-1901

MODERN
TIMES
1902-
NOW

The Falcon Inn has walls made of wattle and daub. Animal poo wasn't only used by tanneries. They sometimes used it to help make daub too!

The houses where the friars lived are revealed in Chester's street names today.

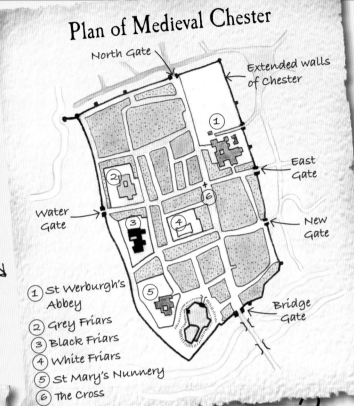

Plan of Medieval Chester

North Gate

Extended walls of Chester

East Gate

New Gate

Water Gate

Bridge Gate

1. St Werburgh's Abbey
2. Grey Friars
3. Black Friars
4. White Friars
5. St Mary's Nunnery
6. The Cross

We'll teach that Llewellyn to pay his taxes!

How do we know?

We know Chester was a busy and wealthy place in the Middle Ages. People like Samuel's father would have made a good living thanks to King Edward's army. In 1277, a Welsh prince called Llewellyn didn't pay his taxes on time and the king decided to do something about it. He gathered a huge army at Chester and they marched into Wales. Edward also ordered castles to be built along the Welsh coast. From 1277 to 1320 many of the engineers and craft workers building those castles would have passed through Chester.

The present Chester Cathedral was an abbey in 1092. Parts of the Norman abbey can still be seen today. We know where the friars lived because the streets in Chester today are named after them, as you can see in the map above.

Tudors and Stuarts

It is market day again and there are stalls laden with fruit and vegetables beneath the walls of St Peter's Church. Most of the crowd are wearing rough woollen clothes but some men wear feathered hats and velvet tunics with slits to reveal glossy satin beneath. Around the Cross, many buildings have changed – some have decorated plasterwork and others are now partly built of red brick which seems to glow in the afternoon sun.

Black and White

Although most buildings were still timber-framed, builders in Tudor Chester began to use new materials. Wattle and daub was now covered with white plaster, made from lime and horsehair, to make it stronger and waterproof. Oak timbers were painted with tar to stop them rotting, so buildings had a striking black and white appearance. Bricks were used to make fireplaces and chimneys. Glass was very expensive and difficult to make, so windowpanes were made small. Plaster was used to make patterns, pictures and shapes on house fronts. Bishop Lloyd's Palace in Watergate Street is covered in symbols and scenes from Bible stories, all made from plaster.

Dissolution

In 1538, Henry VIII, who had declared himself Supreme Head of the Church of England, ordered all abbeys and friaries to be closed and their lands sold off. This became known as the Dissolution of the Monasteries. Friars were no longer seen in the streets of Chester on market days or any other day. This must have been a worrying time for the monks of St Werburgh's monastery but they were lucky. The abbey became Chester Cathedral and the abbot became the first Dean.

Can you name the six wives of Henry VIII?

TUDOR
1485-1603

STUART
1603-1714

GEORGIAN
1714-1837

VICTORIAN
1837-1901

MODERN
TIMES
1902-NOW

Civil War

In 1642, King Charles I had fallen out with Parliament and the two sides gathered armies to fight over who would rule. Most of Chester's people were on the king's side and were called Royalists. On the other side, the commander of Parliament's army in Cheshire was Sir William Brereton. The Royalists managed to stop Brereton from cutting off supplies of food and weapons to Chester in 1643. But when the two sides fought in 1644, Parliament's army won.

In 1646, Brereton led his forces into Chester. Supporters of Parliament were put in charge of the city, which was in a very bad state. Ordinary people were starving and rich Royalists were given big fines. In 1647, a plague spread through Chester, killing 2,000 people and forcing many others to leave. The Civil War ended with Parliament's victory in 1648. This was a low point in Chester's history.

SPOT THIS!

Go to Bishop Lloyd's Palace on Watergate Street and look at the plaster pictures. Can you spot a scene from the story of Adam and Eve?

King Charles's Tower is the place where the king is supposed to have watched a battle on Rowton Moor in 1645. Some say he is more likely to have watched it from the tower of the Cathedral.

People keep calling me a Roundhead but I think my head is perfectly normal.

How do we know?

Parliament's soldiers attacked and broke through the defences at Rowton Moor, 5 kilometres south east of Chester. They brought cannon to St John's churchyard, near the site of the Roman amphitheatre, and fired on the wall near the New Gate. After firing 32 cannon balls they had made an 8 metre-wide hole, which they stormed through. By the Roman Gardens, you can clearly see where the hole was made. Notice the newer stones that have been used to repair the gap.

Coaches and Canals

It is early morning and the cobbles outside the White Lion Inn glisten after overnight rain. Suddenly, there is the sound of horses' hooves and the rattle of wheels. A brightly painted coach appears and stops outside the inn. Some passengers climb inside the coach, while the guard heaves their baggage onto the roof, and others climb up onto basket seats at the back. When everyone is aboard, the driver cracks his whip and the horses spring into life again. The coach gathers speed across the square and down into Northgate Street.

Both the Exchange and the White Lion have now gone. This print shows the Exchange in the middle of the picture and the White Lion Inn is on the left. Can you see the North Gate in the distance?

The City Recovers

During the later years of the 17th century, Chester slowly recovered from the Civil War. Traders and merchants returned to the city.

When news of the Great Fire of London spread, rules were brought in to make sure roofs were made of tile or slate and not thatch. Buildings were still rebuilt in the black-and-white style, but bricks had become less expensive, so were now used more often.

A grand new brick building called the Exchange was built in Chester for meetings of the city council. It opened in 1698 and stood north of the Cross, in a square outside the Cathedral. Chester's largest coaching inn, the White Lion, stood to the west, where horse-drawn coaches regularly left on journeys to London and other cities.

How many more bags, Ma'am?!

The Walls

The 18th century was a peaceful period for Chester. When some other English towns and cities decided that their defensive walls were no longer needed and pulled them down, the people of Chester took a different view. The walls provided a pleasant walk around the city. More and more visitors were arriving to see the Rows and the shops. Large paving stones were laid on the walkways and some of the towers were converted into viewing points and resting stops. The walls became a popular, fashionable place.

The biggest change of all was at the castle, where the outer defences were pulled down and replaced by buildings in the style of Greek temples that can still be seen today.

This is where the Exchange building would be if it was still standing today.

During Georgian times, Chester's medieval towers were replaced with wide stone arches.

SPOT THIS!

Toot, toot! Have you seen this colourful piper in Chester? Look out for him next time you're in Northgate Street. There are a few other little painted figures, too. How many can you spot?

Canals

Over 200 years ago, roads were in poor condition. Carrying goods by canal was a new and fast form of transport. Canals were being built all over the country. The merchants and traders of Chester planned a canal to bring cargoes to their port on the River Dee. It opened in 1779, with a big ceremony by the Water Tower at a place called Tower Wharf.

Twenty years later, the Chester Canal became part of the much longer Shropshire Union Canal. Chester was a busy canal centre, with warehouses for storing cargoes, stables for the horses that pulled the boats and a dry dock for carrying out repairs.

...1779 CEREMONY HELD AT TOWER WHARF TO CELEBRATE NEW CANAL...

19

Let's go back to the year 1820 and hear an imaginary account from Nora, a young girl who lived near the canal and loved to watch the busy scene at Tower Wharf.

I don't know any rude words, Mum, honest!

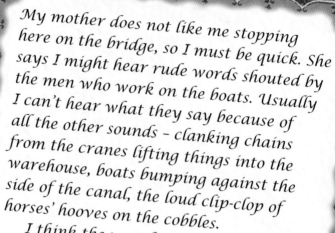

My mother does not like me stopping here on the bridge, so I must be quick. She says I might hear rude words shouted by the men who work on the boats. Usually I can't hear what they say because of all the other sounds – clanking chains from the cranes lifting things into the warehouse, boats bumping against the side of the canal, the loud clip-clop of horses' hooves on the cobbles.

I think the warehouse by the bridge is a lovely building. The boats go in and out of three arches where they are loaded and unloaded. There are boat cargoes piled up on the wharf. I can see stacks of timber and piles of barrels.

My mother says that, one day, we will visit my aunt in Liverpool using the 'Fly boat' which leaves from here. I can see people getting on to the boat. Rich people have servants to carry their luggage. I wonder if I will ever have a big suitcase like that, filled with expensive clothes and hats...

This picture shows Tower Wharf 200 years ago. Do you recognise the warehouse?

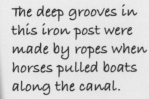

The deep grooves in this iron post were made by ropes when horses pulled boats along the canal.

The locks that take the canal uphill near Northgate Street were dug out of solid rock, using picks and shovels!

This is what the lock at Northgate looks like today.

The workers who built the canals were called navigators, or 'navvies' for short.

I think we might have scared off all the locals!

All the more beer for us!

How do we know?

Although the boats at Tower Wharf carry holidaymakers now, you can still see many of the features that Nora saw. If you stand near the dry-dock on the west side of the canal and look south towards the city centre, you will see that the view hasn't changed much in the last 200 years.

The canal north of Chester was designed by a young engineer called Thomas Telford, who later designed more canals, bridges and railways. He built a warehouse at Tower Wharf in the 1790s that is still known as Telford's Warehouse today. The warehouse was built partly over the canal so boats could be unloaded straight into a bay inside the building. Telford's Warehouse survived a major fire in 2000 and is now a pub, restaurant and arts centre. It is a strong example of Georgian architecture and is a reminder of how busy and successful Chester's port used to be.

Fire, Fire!

It is a dark winter night, but a crowd has gathered in the square. The Exchange is on fire! Flames and smoke shoot out from the roof and windows. There is shouting and jeering as the fire brigade appears, with their hand-pumped engines. The feeble jets of water have no effect on the fire. Soon soldiers from the castle appear. Their engine carries more water but, just as they arrive, the roof of the Exchange caves in with a loud crash and a gush of flames. It is hopeless. This building, which for some years has been Chester's Town Hall, is going to be completely destroyed.

The fire that destroyed the Exchange was widely reported. This picture is from the Illustrated London News.

A New Town Hall

The destruction of the Exchange building by fire in December 1862 was a very dramatic event. The town council saw it as an opportunity, however. They announced a competition to design a new Town Hall, that would not be built on the Exchange site, but on the west of the market square next to a new Market Hall. The White Lion Inn would have to be knocked down, but Chester would have a fine, open square in its centre for the first time.

The competition was won by W.H. Lynn from Belfast and the new Town Hall – the building that we see today – was opened in 1869 in a big ceremony with the Prince of Wales and the Prime Minister.

 SPOT THIS!

This pillar is the only bit of the old Exchange that still stands in Chester today. It's from the front of the Exchange building. Have you seen it?

Building Bridges

The early years of the 19th century saw lots more new developments. A new bridge was built over the river improving the route into Wales. Designed by Thomas Harrison, the Grosvenor Bridge was a graceful stone arch and, at the time of its opening by Princess Victoria in 1832, it was the widest bridge of its kind in the world. Many people thought that the bridge would not stand. To prove them wrong, Harrison had a scale model built using stone blocks of the correct scale size. More inns and hotels were built for visitors, including the Grosvenor Hotel, by the East Gate, which became the premier place to stay for the wealthy and famous.

If you walk down Grosvenor Road, away from the city centre, then turn left into Castle Drive, you can still see Thomas Harrison's scale model of Grosvenor Bridge.

This imaginary character, Thomas, lives with his mother, father and eight brothers and sisters in a two-up, two-down terraced house in Posnett's Court, behind Watergate Street. Although he is only nine years old, he has to work in a nearby bakery because his family is poor. He carries heavy sacks of flour when there is a delivery and sweeps the floor to keep mice away.

One day, on his way to work, Thomas hears people talking about the terrible disaster that has happened the night before on a new railway bridge over the river near the Roodee. He decides this is something he has to see, even if it makes him late for work!

> I give up! Has anyone got a mouse trap?

I rushed home and told Enid and Albert, my younger brother and sister, the news. They wanted to come with me, but I said they were too young. I dashed down Watergate Street and across the racecourse at the Roodee. It was empty that morning, thank goodness! When I got to the river, there was a crowd of people around, but I was able to squeeze to the front because I am only small.

I couldn't believe what I saw! Part of the new Dee Bridge had fallen down and there were railway carriages sticking out of the water. People in small boats were looking in the carriages, probably to see if anyone was stuck inside. I looked again at the bridge and could see that some of the iron girders that held up the rails had fallen into the river. The rails were still there but were all bent and twisted. I heard people saying that someone had been killed in the accident and I wasn't surprised. This was certainly a sight I would never forget!

← A local train fell into the river when part of the new Dee Bridge collapsed in 1847. Five people were killed.

Louise Rayner lived in Chester from 1869 to 1910. Her watercolour paintings show what life was like in Chester in Victorian times.

Many poorer Victorian families like Thomas's would have lived in houses like this in Banners Court.

How do we know?

The Dee Bridge disaster happened on a newly-built line into Wales. We know about it because it was reported in newspapers and magazines at the time. Designed by the famous engineer Robert Stephenson, the new bridge was built of cast iron girders which are strong but can crack and break without warning. After this disaster, steel began to replace cast iron in the design of railway bridges.

The old trades such as leather-making and shipbuilding slowly died out in Chester and people found jobs in shops and hotels. A few new factories were built. Chester had areas of very poor, cramped housing where large families like Thomas's lived in just a few rooms. An area called 'The Courts' behind the new Town Hall was very bad, with as many as ten houses sharing one tap.

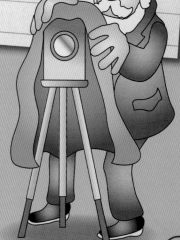

This photo was taken in the 1930s. Soon after that, Banners Court was knocked down and the families were moved to better housing.

25

CELT
500 BC

ROMAN
AD 43-410

ANGLO-
SAXON
AD 450-
1066

VIKING
AD 865-
1066

MEDIEV.
TIME.
1066
1485

Trams, Planes and Motor Cars

A boy in a flat cap trundles a cart full of newspapers along Eastgate Street. On the other side of the road is a horse and trap with a man waiting patiently. There is a clatter of hooves as a horse-drawn cart gets out of the way of a motor car that is noisily leaving the Grosvenor Hotel. In the distance, a tram full of passengers is trundling along; its power coming from electric cables strung high above the street. The pavements are quiet, but there are a few well-dressed visitors walking towards the East Gate and its clock.

The Eastgate Clock was added to celebrate Queen Victoria's Diamond Jubilee.

Eastgate Street

In the late 19th century, a horse-drawn tram system had been used in Chester. In 1903 the trams were updated so they could be run using electric cables, which made them faster and smoother. The trams were quite difficult to move around narrow streets though, and struggled to keep up with the increasing amount of traffic on the roads. Like many tramways in Britain, Chester's trams stopped running in 1930 and were replaced with double-decker buses.

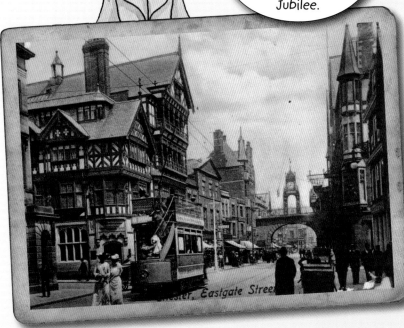

This photograph of Eastgate Street was taken in about 1910. How does it look different from Eastgate Street today?

...1903 Chester trams use electricity...1930 Tram system is closed...

TUDOR
1485-1603

STUART
1603-1714

GEORGIAN
1714-1837

VICTORIAN
1837-1901

MODERN
TIMES
1902-NOW

Chester in the War

Although many people went off to fight in World War Two and some did not return, Chester did not suffer the terrible bombing raids that damaged parts of nearby Manchester and Liverpool. In fact, Chester was considered safe enough for children from Liverpool to be sent to as part of the evacuation in 1939.

During the war years, only 44 bombs fell in or near Chester and little damage was done. The city's big contribution to the war effort was building aircraft to bomb Germany. The aircraft factory at Broughton built thousands of Wellington bombers and over 200 four-engined Lancaster bombers. The same factory now makes wings for Airbus airliners, including the huge A380, which can carry up to 850 people.

Avro Lancaster planes like this one were built in Chester.

SPOT THIS!

Many old buildings were demolished in the 1960s to make way for new roads. The Falcon Inn was saved. If you can find this sign, you're standing right next to the inn!

THE FALCON

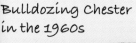
Bulldozing Chester in the 1960s

How do we know?

Most of the tram track in Chester was simply covered over and is still there today, underneath the roads. Part of the track can be seen though, inside the bus depot. In Eastgate Street and Foregate Street, some tram-wire supports are still attached to a few of the buildings.

In the 1950s and 1960s many people thought that Chester should become a more modern place and new roads and office blocks were built. Protests by the newly formed Chester Civic Trust saved buildings like the Falcon Inn from being knocked down, so they are still there for us to see today.

Chester Today and Tomorrow...

Chester's history can be discovered and enjoyed in lots of ways. You can see and touch objects at Grosvenor Museum, visit the Cathedral, walk along the Rows or dress as a Roman and march up Bridge Street. The important thing to remember is that Chester's history is about the people who lived through difficult or exciting or dangerous times – people like Antilianus, Samuel, Nora and Thomas!

I've seen the Rows loads of times but I didn't know they were so old!

The Rows in Chester are unique. There's nothing else quite like them in the whole world!

Chester has the largest zoo in the UK! It puts money towards conservation and the protection of endangered animals like the Black Rhino in Kenya and Tanzania.

CHESTER FOOTBALL CLUB

Chester city football club was founded in 1885. It plays at Deva stadium which opened in 1992. Can you remember where the word 'Deva' came from?

ZOOLOGICAL GARDENS
CHESTER

...1968 JAMES BOND ACTOR DANIEL CRAIG IS BORN IN CHESTER...

Finished in 2009, HQ contains flats, offices, restaurants and a luxury hotel. It's called HQ because it used to be Cheshire Police Headquarters.

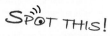

This bronze baby elephant arrived in Chester in 2010. It was made by a sculptor who grew up in India and it was donated to the city by Chester Zoo.

According to records, Chester Racecourse – the Roodee – is the oldest racecourse still being used in England today!

Rhino Mania hit Chester from July to September 2010 as part of the Chester Renaissance Project.

As more and more material goes online, will students still need to go to the University of Chester? Or will they have everything they need to learn at home?

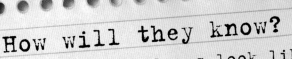

How will they know?

Will Chester always look like it does today? How will future generations know what Chester was like today? The Internet is a great way of recording what Chester is like today. Photos, blogs and stories from tourists can all spread the word about our wonderful Chester. Or maybe you'll be famous one day and put Chester on the map!

Glossary

AD – a short way of writing the Latin words anno Domini, which mean 'in the year of our Lord', i.e. after the birth of Christ.

Amphitheatre – a round open-air theatre, surrounded by seats which rise from the centre so everyone can see and hear.

Archaeologist – a person who studies the past by examining buildings and objects left behind by previous people and cultures.

Barracks – a building where soldiers stay.

Burh – an old Saxon word for a defended settlement. Chester was one of these.

Cemetery – ground set aside for the dead to be buried in.

Cloisters – a quiet, private place such as a monastery or convent. Cloisters can also be the part of a religious building which has a covered walkway open on some sides.

Dock – a place where boats and ships can be tied up safely while they offload their goods or passengers.

Dry dock – a place that can be filled with water and emptied so that work can be carried out on the bottom of a ship. The water can be pumped out and then refilled so the boat can leave once the work is done.

Evacuate – having to leave your home and live somewhere else for safety.

Friar – a male member of a religious order belonging to the Roman Catholic Church.

Georgian era – the time from 1714 to 1830 when any of the four kings called George reigned in England.

Gladiator – a man in Roman times who was trained to fight in an arena, sometimes to the death, usually for entertainment.

Hadrian's Wall – a wall that the Roman Emperor Hadrian ordered to be built across northern England to keep out the North British tribes. Some of the wall survives today.

Hypocaust – a kind of underfloor heating, used in a Roman bathhouse.

Legion – a military unit in the Roman army of between 3,000 and 6,000 men.

Medieval – a period of time in the Middle Ages: roughly from AD 1000 to the 1400s.

Minerva – a Roman goddess of wisdom and healing.

Monastery – a place where monks live and worship.

Praetorium – the home of the commander of a Roman Legion.

Principia – a Roman army headquarters, where their flag was kept.

Relic – an object (or custom) that has survived from the past.

Roundhead – a slang term for someone who supported Parliament and Oliver Cromwell in the English Civil War. They were called this because of their short haircuts.

Royalist – anyone who fought on the side of King Charles I in the English Civil War. Another name for a Royalist was a Cavalier.

Tram – a form of transport used before buses. They ran on rails embedded in the street and were attached to overhead electric cables.

Index

Acknowledgements

In memory of Mike Hardman, Learning Officer at the Grosvenor Museum, whose passion for Chester
and helping children to learn its history was an inspiration to all who knew him.

The author and publishers would like to thank the following people for their generous help:
Jeanne Broadbent and James Pardoe of the University of Chester; Catherine Eales from the History and Heritage Centre;
Kate Harland at the Grosvenor Museum; Caroline Picco of Cheshire Archives; and last but definitely not least,
Elizabeth Royles at the Grosvenor Museum for all of her kind help in providing us with images.

The publishers would like to thank the following people and organisations
for their permission to reproduce material on the following pages:
p4: Grosvenor Museum Cheshire West and Chester Council; p5: Grosvenor Museum Cheshire West and Chester Council;
p6: Take 27 Ltd; p7: Grosvenor Museum Cheshire West and Chester Council, Historic Environment Cheshire West and
Chester Council; p8: Grosvenor Museum Cheshire West and Chester Council; p9: Grosvenor Museum Cheshire West and
Chester Council; p11: Robert Estall photo agency/Alamy; p18: used with permission from Cheshire Records Office;
p20: Chester History and Heritage; p22: Illustrated London News 1863, Chester History and Heritage, Y5/7/5; p24:
Illustrated London News Ltd/Mary Evans; p25: Grosvenor Museum Cheshire West and Chester Council, Chester History
and Heritage; p26: Chester History and Heritage; p27: Kogo/Wikimedia Commons, Chester History and Heritage;
p28: Chester Football Club, Chester Zoo; p29: Ioan Said.

Written by Tony Pickford
Educational consultant: Neil Thompson
Local history consultant: Heather Jones
Designed by Stephen Prosser

Illustrated by Kate Davies, Dynamo Ltd, Peter Kent, John MacGregor, Leighton Noyes and Tim Sutcliffe
Additional photographs by Alex Long

First published by HOMETOWN WORLD in 2010
Hometown World Ltd
7 Northumberland Buildings
Bath BA1 2JB

www.hometownworld.co.uk

Your past
Your now
Your future

Your history4ever

Mmm... Still love chocolate pudding!

My next one's going to have 2 wheels!

Trophy for the trendiest glasses?

I love you too!